REBECCA'S PARABLES

By

Annabelle Lee-Botting

CON-PSY PUBLICATIONS

First Edition

© Ruth Prince
2014

Published by
CON-PSY PUBLICATIONS

P.O. BOX 14,
GREENFORD,
MIDDLESEX, UB6 0UF.

ISBN 978 1 898680 70 3

DEDICATION TO
ANNABELLE LEE-BOTTING
1942 - 2009

Wife, mother, nan, great nan, sister and auntie.

Hub of the family, whose love, guidance and faith kept the spokes together and the wheels of our lives turning. Truly individual, a compassionate human being, loved by all whose lives she touched.

See you at Honeysuckle Cottage.

A dream come true, a promise fulfilled.

Our mother wrote down many teachings she had from Spirit but was unable in her lifetime to have any published. Before she went back home to Spirit, she asked, if the opportunity should arise, would we publish 'Rebecca's Parables' first for her, as it was her dream. Of course, we promised we would.

She was everything to my brother Jamie and I; our soulmate, our Earth angel and guide and now our spirit angel and spirit guide.

This is with all our love for eternity, Mum.

Ruth Prince

Cover illustration of 'Rebecca' by Louisa Hutchison

CONTENTS

A NOTE FROM THE AUTHOR

As a medium, we accept and know of the Eternal Existence of Life. Many times you have heard a medium say, "my guide", meaning, of course, their teacher. I have never disclosed my guide's name, only that she has indeed many times laboured hard to help and teach me.

Through her beautiful guidance, I have learnt and seen the world of our spiritual life. I only wish I could take what I have seen and show it to the world but, of course, none of us may do that, for only you yourself may seek the Kingdom of Heaven.

It is only for us to give to others the things that we are so allowed to give, namely in the many writings that I have been privileged to receive. But this day I pay a tribute to the world of Spirit, the many wonderful helpers who move near to the Earth, that we may hear the voice of God.

Our guides, are disciples who work within the vineyards of Our Father God's House. The house of many rooms and many, many helpers. There are your guardian angels, your healing guides, your guides who may strengthen you with their knowledge; there are many masters who teach many different aspects of knowledge and many helpers whom we are often not even aware of.

But I pay my tribute to a little girl called Rebecca, who is a child who shines with spiritual light. (A helper from the world of Spirit). For in her world of Spirit she works upon the Realms of Great Masters.

Bless you Rebecca for your spiritual teachings.

Annabelle Lee-Botting

MY FATHER'S CHILD

Once, long ago, in the world of 'light', there was a child of great truth. She became the celestial light upon the world of Spirit.

There came the time of great preparing in the Kingdom of Heaven and our Father God asked for many children of great light to go to the Earth world and do His work. Upon this time, He had many children of light who loved him and they laboured hard within the vineyards of heaven, helping the many sick that needed great attendance upon their arrival.

Our Father God became sad that He should see many of His souls of **great light** go back again to the Earth world, for He knew of the sensitivity that would be held within the physical coat that they should have to put on. There was, upon the day that they ascended to Earth, a great allegiance made.

The Father God called together twelve of his angels and said, "These angels shall forever have charge over my children of light, who this day go to the Earth world to do my work, for there shall be many that will mock me, but to you who work in my name then shall my angels ever have charge over you." Our Father God explained to each child the great difficulty of their journey to Earth, for once they had taken on the coat of Physical Matter, the world of light would not be easy to find.

"Dear children," said our Father God, "you go to the Earth world this day **knowing** of me, but when thy mother of life gives to you your coat of physical life, to see me will be the furthest from your mind. For you will be on planet Earth and will play with the young of Earth and see your life with Earth eyes. So to find me will not be easy, but when you are passed from your childhood days I shall try and awaken you. But still you will find it difficult, for you will not want to know me.

9

"Some of you will take many times for me to awaken you from your sleep within the physical coat. So you see, children, why this day I am sad, but when you open the 'eye' of your temple so shall I give my angels charge over thee. Many times you will be lost, many times you will cry out in the wilderness of the Earth plane, but I promise you that my angels shall ever open the doors of truth, that you may be fed. Now, some of you shall walk in high places and some of you shall walk in lowly places. Some of you shall have a colour that shall be different, some of you shall be of great scholarships and some of you shall not; many coats of disguise shall you wear, but each of you shall have the **light** that you came to Earth with.

"It matters not how long it may take to awaken you, for you are my children. Each of you shall give something of me to help your brothers and sisters of the Earth."

And so it was that day, that many souls of great light came to the Earth world. Some became teachers, some became servants and some became saints. But **truly** was the Kingdom of Heaven opened, for the many who came to the Earth gave a great light so that the darkness of the Earth world became lifted away. When our Father's angels saw the **light**, they rejoiced. For they were then able to move near to the Earth world and help.

The angels' names were: Love, Joy, Peace, Humility, Jealousy, Anger, Passion, Birth, Death, Danger, Truth and Mercy. They were given a gate that each in turn they would sit by, so they would show them how to overcome their problems. For, you see, the Father God knew that the Earth plane had need to be taught. The angels were **all of truth** but each one knew that the Earth's thoughts were greatly in need of help. So, therefore, each angel was placed where they could help.

The first child who came to the Earth world was the greatest light of all. Our Father God treasured her above all else for she was Life. Our Father God knew when He sent her to the Earth that He had given His favourite child, for she was Perfection.

When He sent her to the Earth, He knew she would be the most ignored of all His children, for the angels could help and teach and forever be near. But His favourite child would be used and taken for granted. And our Father God knew that she could not return and sit with Him until all people upon Earth could see that Life came from the Kingdom of Heaven.

But now the aeons of years have passed and the angels have around them many other helpers. And the child of great Life is beginning to show to the Earth that their physical coat is but a disguise; a cloak of convenience that you put on to see the Earth world.

One day the child of great truth, who is known as Life, will return to the Kingdom of God and the angels shall throw open the gates that they sit by, for all Mankind shall be the sons and daughters of God. For His most treasured of angels – You – shall sit by him, and Life shall at last become his again.

May God forever go with you and all children of the Earth world.

THE CITY OF LIGHT

Once, long ago, in the village of Bethel, near Israel, lived a family who happily tilled a small piece of land for the yearly harvest which gave unto them their daily bread. They had a few swine, which they used to barter in the marketplace for the few garments they may require.

The family were of four - Father, mother and two sons, Arab and Melca.

Melca was the eldest son and helped his father with the daily chores. Arab was a sickly child who had not been born with great strength, so his mother nurtured and fed him each day that he may grow strong.

There came the time in the passing years that Arab wished to help his brother Melca; he longed to go to the market square and barter with the swine that had been taken so that he too could be strong and help his father and mother. Arab begged his mother to let him go but his mother knew his health was not good. "When you are a little stronger you may go," she said, "but for now you must grow in health."

Arab asked his mother why he was so weak in his body and why Melca was so strong. His mother was a very holy mother who believed that Arab was given to her to nurture and love and that if she prayed for help and guidance from God that one day her son would become strong in health.

She explained to Arab that long ago God had spoken to her and that deep within her heart she knew that a city of great light was within the Earth world and that one day she would set out upon a journey to find the city of light.

For with the vision that she had seen, she had seen great **glistening temples** with colours that cascaded down from them and in the centre of the courtyard, lay the most wonderful **healing streams**.

Arab sat and listened to his mother and said, "Why can't we go now and find this place called The City of Light, Mother?"

"Because you are not yet strong enough to climb the mountain that hides The City of Light," said his mother. As the years passed Arab grew into a fine young man, with the most gentle of natures; he had an understanding that was very wise. And in all life he saw God.

Although he was a fine young man in his nature, he was unable to do the many things he had so dreamed of doing. His legs were weak and he needed crutches so that he may walk. His brother, Melca, was a good brother but he did not understand the limitations of his brother Arab. Off Melca would go to the market square caring not that Arab had never been able to go. But now the time had come and Arab had reached the age of two score years and ten.

Arab had spent many years learning from his mother and father. His mother had given to Arab his own strength, for with the passing of time Arab had a faith so strong that he had accepted the trials of his life.

One night, whilst sitting around the open fire, he surveyed the beauty of that night. The stars were shining and sending the sparkling gifts of peace down upon the ground that Arab sat upon. He looked at his mother, who had become older with time and said to her, "Mother, thank you for your love, thank you for all you have taught me."

"Oh, my son," she said, "I have done nothing, it is you who have grown strong."

"But Mother, I let you down, you wanted so much for me to walk and play like my brother Melca."

"Yes, my son, I had hoped you would walk, I had hoped you could do many things that you so wanted, but my son you are now **stronger** than I could ever have hoped for. You have the strength of faith and love so deeply within you that now you have to climb that mountain that hides the City of Light.

Arab pondered upon the words his mother spoke. "Yes," said his mother, "the strength I speak of is not a strength that moves your legs, but the strength that overcomes the barriers that are put within your pathway of life."

Now Arab had grown tired and began to sleep as the stars grew brighter. As he fell into his sleep he heard a voice say, "Arab, take your crutches and cast them into the fire that you sit by." Arab awoke and yet was still asleep and said, "I cannot burn my crutches and my father laboured hard to make them." But the voice said again, "Take the crutches and burn them." Arab heard the voice and looked hard to see who it was but only could he see a light, a small light, that seemed far away.

He got up from where he sat and pulled himself towards the fire and threw his crutches into the flames. As they burnt, the flames grew and became a great light. Arab asked what now he should do. "Cast now your body into the light that you see," said the voice. Arab did not hesitate, for he knew this light was a light he had often seen but never had he seen it so bright. As he walked towards the fire he felt no heat, neither did it scorch him; he walked forward into the light with a strength so great that faith led him.

And then he saw the most beautiful City of Light amidst the fire. And a voice said to him, "You cast away the limitations of your physical body, you gave to me your total faith and love. Then so did you by that strength climb the 'mountain' that led you to my City of Great Light."

Arab felt his soul anointed with the waters of healing that lay within that city. And the voice said to him, "Go, my son of the Earth and tell many of what you have found. **For this night have we become one**."

Arab awoke from his sleep and the dawn was breaking. He glanced around to see if he had been dreaming. There were his crutches and he looked down to his withered legs.

He sat for a moment pondering upon his vision. "No," he said, "I know it was real. I know, now I am awake, that I did see that City of Great Light, for that city lies within me, I am my Father God's Temple. All that my Father so wishes, so we can become." With faith, he stood up and walked towards his mother's bed. When his mother awoke she cried out, "Arab, where are you crutches?"

"Mother, I have no need, for with my strength I can walk. I have no longer any need to rely on them." His mother held him closely and said, "You found the strength to climb that mountain and you saw that City of Light, didn't you, my son?"

"Yes, my beloved mother, thank you for leading me towards it. Now I understand that, although we may think many times that a burden is too great, if we overcome that burden with acceptance, strength and faith then surely shall we see all that God has given unto us. For the City of Great Light is ours to enter. With love, that we may raise above all Earthly limitations by the way of faith."

THE ROSE

There once was a man who laboured hard for a living; he had, since a small boy, learnt to till the land. Now he was older his knowledge was great; he could look to the east and to the west to attune with the weather. Sometimes the winds would blow from the north and south, but within the very breath of that wind he knew what to plant and what to reap. With the years of growing, he had indeed become a fine gardener.

Now, within the city of Rome there were many grand houses, with families whose wealth far outspun the gardener's dreams, for he lived outside the city gates and tilled the small piece of ground he lived by. He had a wife and three daughters who all helped to dig and turn the soil so that their yearly crop may grow.

But there came a time that a great 'Command' was made from the city of Rome that all people who lived outside the city walls were to bring their families within the city market square.

Now, the gardener gathered his family around him and said, "We must obey, for if not we shall surely be punished." Off they set that morning, joining the many others that too had to obey the Roman law. There were many that met that day within the market square.

Finally, a great trumpet sounded and all noise ceased. Up drove a fine carriage, drawn by many mighty horses and from the carriage many soldiers appeared. One, who was the leader, said, "This day, by the order of the city of Rome, we make a proclamation that your yearly harvest is to become ours. Each one of you may have one quarter of what you till but, by the order of Rome, you must give to the city the rest."

Now, the gardener knew that, like the rest of the people gathered there, they would not be able to live. So he stepped forward and said to the soldiers, "We beg of you, sir, to be merciful, for if we give to you that much how then shall we be able to feed our own families?" The soldier came forward and smote the face of the gardener and said, "You shall do as we say, you who dare speak out of turn." The crowd walked slowly out of the city gates to return to their small villages.

On the way they all spoke of many things and asked the Gardener, who seemed so wise, what should they do. "Go home and till your lands, worry not yet about the new decree. I will give it thought and send for you all when we can see a way." The gardener went into his small house and sat with his wife and three daughters, who in turn asked what should they do. He replied, "Do not worry, for is there not bread and wine upon our table? Are we not full this day? We do not hunger, let tomorrow come."

Now, the house was quiet, so the gardener got up from his bed and walked out into the small field nearby. As he sat there he thought about the many gifts that nature had given to him. The harvest which gave to him his daily bread. How the sun, the rain, the wind and the earth gave freely, that all man may survive.

He decided to pray and went down upon his knees. "Dear Father God, I thank you for all you have given to the Earth world, that all man may live, but my Father God we live not only on the Earth world that you created but we live with many who think differently, many who want even our small amount of food. Please Father, tell me what to do, show me why."

The gardener felt a great presence and he heard a voice say unto him, "My son, all that is within the earth was given freely that you all should live. It is true that time and time again Man takes for himself what he wants and cares not that his brothers and sisters may starve. But hearken not to the voice of greed, for I shall turn one day the tabernacles of greed into the City of Peace. Go this night to all you can gather and tell them that if they gather in the name of peace so shall they be shown the way."

The gardener got up from his knees and went in and woke his wife and three daughters. "Quickly, we must gather as many as we can together."

Off they went to the north, south, east and west until by morning many were gathered together.

The gardener stood in the early morning sunrise and spoke to the many who had gathered there, saying, "This day, my friends, we shall join as brothers and sisters and worship our Father God, for nothing is greater than the truth of prayer."

All the masses that were gathered bent their heads in prayer. "Dear God, you givest unto us our daily bread, we thank thee. Please show us the way, that our fellow man may also share and not take from us our food, for it is our life." There appeared a great vision and the earth began to tremble and the skies shone with many colours.

The gardener stood as many fell to the ground, saying, "Do not fear, for does not God speak to thee?" And there before him stood the most wonderful soul. The gardener fell to his knees. "Oh, my beloved, who are thee?" he said. "I am the keeper of my Father's sheep and you who this day honour and worship God, do you not see that by thy prayer, by thy joining together, that you have indeed become an army of soldiers in his name? Rise my sons and daughters of the Earth world and **see**".

Each person rose from the ground and beheld the most beautiful sight. For there, amidst the garden that they had gathered in, was the most beautiful rose. The petals were many and as you looked upon it so did it hold a thousand different colours.

"Now," said the gardener to all who were gathered there, "Now we see the beauty of our prayer. All go home and till your lands, do not fear your tomorrows, but each evening we will join in prayer, giving thanks for what we have received, knowing that there shall be a way shown."

The days and weeks passed and the rose stood within the garden as fresh and beautiful as it was first seen.

Then came the day that the soldiers sent word that they required three-quarters of the yearly harvest. Now all gathered within the garden with their carts full of the yield from the harvest.

Up drove the army of soldiers towards the gathering crowds into the garden to take the awaiting harvest. As the leader of the army got down from his horse, he glanced upon the beauty of the rose that glistened and sparkled with light.

"Oh," he said to the gardener, "hiding that from the city of Rome are you? Well, we want three-quarters of your harvest and that includes the rose." He drew his sword from his side and lifted it to smite the rose in half. But as his sword came down toward it, the rose shone a light so bright that the soldier was blinded by its vision. He looked away and laughed and said, "What trick is this then gardener?"

He again lifted his sword to smite the rose in half and again the light became so bright that he could not see. He became a little afraid and said to his soldiers, "Go forward and smite this rose." The army of soldiers walked towards the rose with their swords drawn. As they lifted their swords together they too were blinded by its light. And a voice said, "Is it not enough that you wish to take your brothers' and sisters' bread? Is it not enough that you should see them hungry? You cannot take from them this **rose** for it is Me. I am within all, but this rose is my children's love, this rose is their temple, for from Me did it come and from Me it was given. You may take the things that rot, you may take the things that decay, but you cannot touch that which is beyond your **vision**.

19

The soldiers fled and returned to the city of Rome. And the gardener and the masses who had gathered were able to keep their yearly crops. And never did the rose die, for from prayer it was ever fed, to grow within the Earth world, for the many, many more who joined together within the garden of Gethsemane, that peace, love and truth shall always overcome the turmoils of the Earth world.

THE WATERS OF PEACE

Once, long ago, in the city of Judea, the waters of Babylon flowed. The waters of Babylon were greatly relied upon, as the many who lived by it needed to drink and feed their oxen.

Now, in the city of Judea lived many great people; there were many scholars and teachers there who spent many days within their synagogues. One of the great teachers was called Abraham and he was a master, for within him was great wisdom. Many that visited the city would call upon him for his counselling.

He was a man of great strength and had learnt many things from the wise masters who came before him. Abraham could see truth mapped within the stars; he could see truth in travel within the human mind. Abraham was a kind man who embraced the many different teachings of guidance, for he understood the Jew, the gentiles and the apothecaries, who were many in that time.

Within each man he saw Truth, for he knew that if a man sought knowledge of guidance then surely he was seeking God. There came upon the city a great famine, for the waters of Babylon began to cease their flow, so no longer did it reach the walls of the city of Judea. Abraham was consulted by many as to what they should do, for soon they would thirst and their oxen should die.

Abraham, being a wise man, told the many to go home, for soon the city should see much water. All the kings asked of him, "How can this be? For you see that our rivers no longer flow, you see that the sun is so hot, it melts the very earth." But Abraham replied, "Go home, for soon the waters will flow."

Abraham closed the doors of his temple that night and consulted the Oracle of All Life, our Father God. Within his temple was a great dome that you could look out into the night. It revealed to him the sun, the moon, the stars; all the beauties of the Earth world were never shut away from his vision.

He sat at his table of maps and studied the tides of the many rivers. Tiberias was a river that ran far from the north and from the mouth of that river so did many rivers spring from.

The many scriptures of wisdom were before him, so he pushed aside the teachings of the Oracle, which were the study of the Earth world and opened the scriptures of God. The scroll he chose came from the old masters of wisdom and contained many of the Greek mysteries, called Mythology.

Within these teachings there were many gods, as some were, gods of rain, gods of earth and gods of water. But Abraham, being a wise man, knew that the teachings were to show only one god, but the many gifts that God so gave so then did man worship. The Water Bearer, was known by Pythagoras because he was the master of great wisdom. Pythagoras was a Greek master of great light, who gave unto man many teachings.

He showed within his writings the scrolls of many different gods, but each one leading to one god. The Water Bearer was Pythagoras' favourite because he realised that heat and light and earth was for Mankind's existence. But that water was also needed, not only to feed Mankind, but to flow upon the Earth for balance.

Abraham continued to read many of the scrolls that lay before him. When he glanced to his side and saw a great light, now being a soothsayer, he understood the presence of spirit. So, he said, "Who are you, my friend?" "I am the voice you wish to hear, for do you not want to know of the waters of Babylon? Have you not consulted the Oracle of the Earth and have you not read the many teachings that the great masters of wisdom have given unto you?"

"Yes," said Abraham, "I have and I find that Pythagoras knew a great deal about God. For in all things he saw light, in all things he mathematically saw rhythm. He, therefore, understood the Earth world, the elements, all their needs, all their strength and in the stars he also saw wisdom. So he too was a wise man, but above all else he loved only one God.

"The Water Bearer of life givest unto all thirsty, for nothing may grow without it. You may have the earth, you may have the air, you may have the sun, the moon and the stars, but none can flourish without the other."

So Pythagoras considered the Water Bearer first. Although each work in rhythm with each other, all that Pythagoras learnt was firstly mapped from the water of the Earth and there flowed that he may chart the mysteries of the universe.

"Well, my friend," said Abraham, "I thank you for your guidance and wisdom. Can you now help me to unfold the mysteries of our river Babylon?"

"What you must do," said the soul of great light, "is ask why the water does not flow freely and secondly seek the truth of its use and then surely shall you understand".

Now Abraham was a wise man, full of love and wisdom. He placed around himself a cloak of love and off he set upon a journey towards the river of Babylon. Upon his way he stopped and passed many blessings to the lame and sick who lay upon the pathways that he walked. He stopped to rest as his legs grew weary, the stars of the night shone brightly and the moon was a quarter full.

Being a soothsayer, he understood by the moon and stars that the tide waned and ebbed according to her fullness of the turning. He studied the depth of the stars and understood that that night would bring a great storm. He gathered his cloak of love around him and hurried back to the city of Judea.

23

Quickly, he knocked upon the doors of many and said, "Quickly, my children, you must be prepared, the river shall flow so fast that it shall break from the banks that hold her. Now the kings who had many times consulted Abraham had waited for an answer, but they chose to think that Abraham could not see the changing of the coming waters.

"Go home soothsayer, consult your Oracle, for your god has deserted us. You cannot turn the tides, neither does your god hear you."

The Jews and the gentiles had often disagreed and the soothsayers of wisdom were often abused, for they, many times, had tried to show there was but one God, that all within the Earth came from him. And only was their learning different.

Abraham went quickly to his temple of worship and asked God what he should do, for now no one wished to hear the wisdom that he had given.

"Go my son," said a voice. "Gather as many of you as you can and stand upon the Mount of Olives, that you may be kept safe."

Abraham went gathering as many who would come. Now, amongst the many who gathered with him were many children, some of Jews, some of gentiles. They went with him to the top of the mount and there sat until the great storm broke. The waters of the great rivers flowed and rushed past them, with the wind howling with joy.

Many were afraid, but Abraham said to them, "Be not afraid, for God has all in His keeping. For the Earth world is His and all therein." The morning began to break and the sun rose and shone upon the waters that flowed below. The howling wind had turned into a soft gentle whisper.

Now Abraham looked down upon the city of Judea and many were sorely lost. For the storm of that night had cast many away. But upon the time of sunrise they were able to walk back in to the city and the river flowed within its banks.

All who walked with Abraham were dismayed; many who had stayed were still within the city and were kept from harm. They rushed towards Abraham, throwing themselves upon their knees, saying, "Abraham you knew! This strange knowing, this soothsaying, the Oracle, is indeed to be taken seriously. What can we do to find the truths that you see in the stars, in the earth, in this one God of yours?" Abraham said, "Children from the city of Judea, one day a great Master shall appear, the Son of God, he shall be called. So go this day and prepare for his coming, do homage to his Father.

"For God gave to you the earth, the sea, the sun and your very life. Thus it is by these gifts that you live. Do not see the gifts only as of use, but see them as gifts of beauty not to be abused. Do not think that as the ebbs of the Earth turn that it is only for you to choose to use until it is no longer there. But see the gifts of God.

"See, the controller is the essence of all life. Do not wait until you have to cry out in thirst. But bless the very things that you have in your daily life. Listen to the voice of reason. Listen to the Son of God, for he comes to teach many things. The mountain that you this day sat upon shall one day be the Mountain of Truth. For he shall, the Son of God, show to you the truth of the Eternal Life. And still will the water of the Earth world flow and still you will not see the Holy Water of Peace until again the river of Babylon shall cease to flow. And yet again shall you all cry out to be shown the way. And yet shall even another Master teach you until you shall see the Water Bearer of all life is God."

JEWELS IN THE MIST

Once, long ago, in the city of Judea, lived a girl called Marcia. She was an orphan so had no father or mother to guide her through her life. She had only known the herding of swine and the feeding of swine and at nightfall she would fall asleep upon the wayside, beneath the stars.

Often Marcia would only be rewarded for her daily tasks by the receiving of a crust of bread and a sip of the segments of wine that had been left as empty by the other serfs.

Marcia had reached the age of seven and within those years could only vaguely remember the soft, warm love of her mother and father. For at the age of two her mother and father had been taken as slaves and sold within the city. Marcia's mother, upon the approach of the slave seekers, hid her baby child within a woven basket that lay in a small room. The baby made no sound as she was in sleep.

Marcia's parents that day were sold and taken into bondage to serve the ways of the rich, who sought many servants for their own pleasures. As the evening of that day grew to dusk the baby awoke and cried, for thirst and hunger was upon her. Passing by the croft door was an old lady, who had long past childbearing years. The old lady was a beggar and had no fixed abode to live. As she heard the muffled cry of the child, she entered the croft and searched for the child.

The old lady lifted the lid of the woven basket and beheld the beauty of the baby child Marcia. The old lady knew of the hunger of the baby and so searched to find a few morsels of food. Then, knowing of the times that were upon the city of Judea, the old lady knew that the baby's parents would not return, so she set out to put the croft in order and upon the sleep of the baby, gasped upon her beauty and decided that from that moment on she would love and nurture the child.

The days and weeks passed until the passing of a year. The old lady had begged many times for a few vitals of food for the child, but the people who were within the city did not take kindly to the many beggars who asked for alms.

Now, Marcia had grown and could now help with the asking of vitals. Each morning they would set off towards the market square and sit upon the steps that led to the great synagogue and laying down the plate of asking, would look to the rich to have mercy upon them. The old lady had reached the age of four score years and her body had become frail and weary of life.

As they sat that day upon the temple steps, a great army of soldiers appeared within the market square. They had come to barter and give very little for the food they needed to fortify their hungry armies.

The soldiers had drunk of far too much wine and their heads were not of their own. There broke out amongst the crowds a great fight and many lay dead and wounded.

The old lady had sat upon the steps, holding Marcia very tightly near her, when one of the soldiers rode towards them and pulled the child from the old lady's arms. The old lady got up and cried out in anger but the soldiers rode towards her and cut her down. The small child, Marcia, was thrown to the wayside and left to survive alone.

Marcia sat at the side of the swine, recalling the memories of that day and how sadly she missed the old lady's love. All she had known since the passing of time was the wandering with the swine and to receive a crust of bread. There were no shoes upon her feet and only rags upon her back and her frail body was in great need of food.

Marcia fell into sleep and awoke later to the sound of voices talking. And then towards her walked two of the swine owners. "Come on child," said one. "You are worth a sovereign or two and you're no good to us." Off Marcia was taken by the slave buyers. Marcia only was worth a few pieces of gold and was bought to serve in a great house.

As the years passed, Marcia grew strong and very beautiful. She was happy, for no longer was she hungry and did not sleep now with the swine. The servants of the house grew in love for Marcia, as she was a child who showed great wisdom. Her nights were spent telling many wonderful stories to the servants, who were her friends.

Marcia never quite understood where the great stories came from, but it seemed as though she sat for a moment and then heard what she was to say. Now, the soothsayers of that time heard of Marcia and understood the great gifts that she so had. They went to the master of the house and asked that they may enter Marcia into the tabernacles of knowing.

The master of the house was a wise man and had many times consulted the Oracle of God from the soothsayers' tabernacles. He blessed Marcia and that day gave to her her freedom that she may become a servant to God.

Within the tabernacles of truth, Marcia was schooled of many things and from her tongue of speaking grew many, many wise teachings. The soothsayers loved Marcia and indeed understood that she had come to the Earth world as a bearer of many gifts.

Now, there came a time that a great king asked for an oracle consultation. He drew up outside the tabernacle in his great carriage, drawn by fine and mighty horses. The servants who had escorted him fell to their knees as he walked towards the tabernacle. Marcia was chosen that day to consult the Oracle of Truth, that she may guide the king to the answers he sought.

The king walked toward Marcia with his mighty power of authority and asked her to commence. Marcia sat and looked into the heart of the king and was saddened by the truths she saw that lay within him. He said, "Come now child, get on with it, I have not all day. Ask your God why the very thing I want so much does evade me. Does he not know that I need an heir to my throne?"

Marcia bent her head in wisdom and asked that she may receive guidance and she spoke to the king saying, "This day you ask why a child has not been given to you, this day you ask why you have been denied the very thing you need."

"That's right," said the King. "Now don't hang around child, consult your God." Marcia fell into a sleep and a voice from her mouth spoke.

"My son, you ask of me the truth and yet if I speak to you of truth, you shall wish to slay me," said the voice. "But I shall say to you, you take from the Earth all pleasures you seek, you take from the Earth your life, but you give to the Earth nothing, your greed and desires and wishes are all that matter and you dare ask why you have no child."

The king rose in anger and asked who dare speak to him in this way. "I do," replied the voice. "Now go this day and give to the Earth, give to your servants' lives, give to those who have nothing and return when you have done so."

Marcia awoke from her sleep and the King was sorely angry. "How dare you mock me, child," said the king.

"It was not I," said Marcia, "but the voice of truth." The king left that day and bid the soothsayers farewell. Some time passed and the king sent a messenger to the tabernacles of truth and asked that Marcia should visit his home.

Upon her arrival at the palace, Marcia was greeted by the king, who was sad within his heart that he had no child and his wife had passed over into the world of Spirit. Oh, he had many servants, but none could bear his child. With all his wealth, he had become now sad that his life was so empty.

Marcia sat and told him many stories of wisdom, that he may learn truth. The months passed and Marcia was asked every day to visit the palace.

With the passing of time the king began to see the errors of his ways and mellowed in his thoughts. The servants were better cared for and the tables of food were shared with many more. And Marcia taught to him the truth that he may understand and love God.

The passing of one score years had gone and the king no longer wanted the wealth, nor power, that he had known. He sought peace and sharing with all the people of the city. And many who were homeless were given shelter and fed.

Marcia and the king fell in love, for between them lay the love for God. Between them now lay great wisdom. The soothsayers of the tabernacles were invited to join in counselling and asked to give their blessings upon their marriage. Marcia dressed for the day of the ceremony in the white of truth and gathered in her hands were flowers of forget-me-nots; they had been collected by the children of the city.

The great moment arrived and the day was full of rejoicing. The evening gathered as they took leave of the day and quietly sought peace together. As they talked of many things, they embraced each other with the love that lay between them.

One year later, on the night of Christmas, a small child was born to them both. Marcia and the king grew old and Marcia grew weary of life, as the child grew in strength. He was a fine man, called David. David knew of the gifts of his mother and the strength of his father, so with the ageing of David came great wisdom and wealth.

David opened a tabernacle of truth and the palace became a great place of consulting the Oracle. With the passing of time, his father and mother went to the world of Eternal Life, for David knew of these things. There came a time that

David set upon a great journey to seek the Holy One who he had heard many stories of.

Jesus of Nazareth he was called; the Son of God, said many people. When David met Jesus, he listened to the many teachings and felt at one with Jesus. David was asked by Jesus to follow him and so did they set out upon a great journey in life.

Now, David wondered what he should do with his lands and his wealth and Jesus said to him, "Go and give back to the Earth world that all people may share the jewels of your wealth." David loved Jesus and understood the words of guidance he had been given. He set off towards the palace and bid his servants to come and said, "This day I give to you my wealth. That I may walk with the master Jesus."

There came a loud voice across the city of Judea: "Welcome, my son, you have given to the Earth the things that are hers; you have given to me the love and truth that shall give to you more treasures in the Kingdom of Heaven than tenfold of jewels upon Earth could give you. Your mother walked with swine and yet loved me. Your father walked with kings yet loved me. You walk with my son and give back the powers of the Earth that you may walk with me into the City of Truth. For the jewels of life are but a mist veiling the truth from all men. This day in the city of Judea, the veil of life begins. For the mist of truth shall be lifted that you may help the people of Earth world understand that the trials of all life were to find The Jewels of Truth."

THE PRINCE OF PEACE

Once, long ago, in the city of Judea, lived an old man. He was a tinker in that land and spent many hours at the different trades he had learnt. He sat one evening by the light of his lamp, stitching at an old oil cloth that was being prepared by him to fit a small fishing boat that had been shored nearby. The work that had been given to him would bring to him enough silver to purchase a few vitals that he needed to service his daily needs.

The old man was a kindly soul, who had spent many years in service to his fellow man. He had little to show for the many hard years of labour, for looking around him, beneath the soft glow of his lamp, were only a few necessary vessels for his daily use. Melca was a well worn old man, now having reached the age of three score years. But as he stitched upon the sail cloth within his hand, his thoughts turned to the past years.

The time was late but he worked knowing that his work must be completed in time, that he may receive payment the following day. His eyes grew heavy as the night grew long. Melca came from a family of four children; there were two brothers, Isiah and Melma and a sister, Reba and himself. He recalled the joys of his past childhood and how his mother and father had laboured hard that they all may have food enough to live. With the passing of time his two brothers had died within the wars of the Roman armies. Melca thought about the youth of his brothers and how young they had been upon their passing from Earth life.

His mother and father had long passed with the ageing of their time. His sister, Reba, was a lovely child, who had not lived past the time of one score year. Melca's thoughts passed through that night until his work was done. His eyes now had grown tired and the morning light was breaking. He reached forward to pluck the light and rest for a while.

The sun was just rising and from the east was a rich glow of many colours coming over the far distant hills. Just as his eyes were closing, his thoughts pondered upon the years that had passed.

"Why me, just to be left now on this Earth? Why, when all I do is labour upon the needs of others? My two brothers are far braver than I and did much for their cause. My dearest sister knew so little of life and had the kindest heart. Here am I, unworthy of many things. I cannot carve my name upon a tablet of stone, neither can I understand the writings of wise men. Why have I been such an empty vessel? So little have I done, that many others have done."

To the rising of the sun, he gazed upon its beauty and said, "I thank thee our Lord, that you have given such beauty to the Earth world. I wish that I could have given of myself much more. For it is only with my hands that I may labour upon this Earth. But within my heart it was my wish to have accomplished much more, that I may have at least left something for my fellow man to remember me by. Something that would have honoured thee Lord. For you give all to the Earth world and I give to thee nothing in return; only my life as a tinker. Would it not have been better if I had long gone and others more worthy than I had more score years upon thy Earth?" As he turned to close his eyes in sleep, a bright light appeared across the hills within the far off valley.

"Oh my son," said a voice, "do you not see the joy you have done unto me? Do you not know that you have walked amongst men as a Prince of Peace? For neither do you chastise me, for neither do you repent to me. For you do not say, 'Oh lord, what have you done? For you do not say, 'Lord, you have betrayed me'. You do not ask why you cannot do or have.

For you have walked upon your road of life bearing a service unto your brothers and sisters of the Earth world. In all life you have seen truth, in all the passing of your loved ones you have grieved only of their young life gone. You do not say unto me, 'Lord, thou hast cheated me', you ask that you may serve your fellow man and wish that you were able to give more unto the Earth.

"But I say unto you, my son, great is the gift you bear within your Earth life, for humble is your heart. Truth is in your tongue. Peace is in thy breast. To you who walks his Earth life, you shall do more for me than many. For to love me in all your humilities, for to love me in all your times of need, then indeed are you a prince amongst many men. That you spread to all Mankind my love. For in you, my son, so shall they see me also."

THE CARPENTER OF JOY

Long ago, in the city of Jerusalem, lived a carpenter and his family. The carpenter had seven children, six were sons and one was a daughter. The daughter was the eldest child, so had laboured hard with her mother in the helping of the raising of her brothers.

The carpenter laboured hard within his workshop, making and repairing the many tools of that day. His sons had all now grown and were tilling upon a small piece of land that lay nearby.

The morning of that day was near to the time for the carpenter to take rest and eat, as the sun was high upon that morning. The heat of that day sorely tried his patience, as nearby to his workshop were many wheels that were in need of repair. And within the heat of the day the carpenter found it hard to cope on his own.

Now, in the nearby field, he caught sight of his eldest son, Mennorr. So, calling across to him then came his son to help. His son teased his father and ruffled his hair in play, saying, "Come now father, are not your muscles as strong as they were?" Great laughter broke out between them and much that day was done and grateful was the carpenter for the help from his son.

The evening came and then the setting of the sun. Each child returned from the fields of harvest and before them all was the table of thanksgiving that had been prepared by their mother and sister.

The house they lived in was a house of prayer, so each knew before sitting at the table of thanksgiving that they must remove their shoes and wash their hands from the tasks of the day. There was, from the yard, great noise as each son was washing and teasing each other, as each one wished to go before the other. The carpenter peered from the door and called upon his sons to stand to a form of order, as if they continued as they were none would succeed in finishing in time, for the table was prepared.

A little while had passed and at last all sat at the table of thanksgiving. The carpenter bid all to join him in prayer. With head bent forwards, he said, "We thank thee God for all thy mercies, for all thy love. For this day you have given unto us our daily bread. We thank thee for our harvest of food upon this table of thanksgiving." The food was then served and great joy came forth from the mouths of all gathered there.

As the evening grew so did the carpenter take himself to bed, for the day had been long and he had grown weary. Upon his time of rest he knelt in prayer, to thank the Lord for his joy, for his life and for the fullness of his life. He was a man of much knowing and in all life he saw the Lord.

Upon his rising the next morning, he felt troubled in his heart, for a strange dream had befallen him. All that day he pondered upon the dream, at what he should do, for in his dream there had been the vision of many angels. He gathered to him his sons and the eldest son, Mennorr, he asked what he should do. His son never questioned what the dream was but fairly said that his father was a wise man who had lived a life of truth, so therefore must do what he had been guided to do.

The carpenter bid his family farewell, for he must set out upon a journey; when he had completed his task he would again return. His sons and daughter wished him God speed and a safe journey. His wife begged for him not to go, for she was sorely afraid.

Now the carpenter was to go far into the mountains, this much he knew to do. For seven days he travelled, walking upon the stony harsh ground that led towards the mountains. The sun was high on the seventh day, so he sat upon the wayside to rest. As he sat a pilgrim of people approached, weary were they for they had travelled far. They drew near unto him and stopped, saying, "Oh holy one, you are here, just as was prophesied."

The carpenter looked upon the leader of the pilgrims and said, "Where are you bound?" "We are bound to find the Promised Land, where peace and truth can be found," said the leader. "I have been told that we shall find the Holy One, who shall lead us, at the foot of the hills, as you sit."

The carpenter was troubled by the words they spoke, but he still held within him the strange dream that must be fulfilled. He turned to the leader of the pilgrims and said, "I shall lead you upon the journey I take, but then I must leave you."

The children gathered at the carpenter's feet and begged for him to guide them to their promised land. "I can only lead you where I am going," he said, "and then I must leave you." The carpenter rose to his feet and walked now forwards, with the pilgrims following. As the evening grew to dusk so did they draw near unto the mountains.

"In the morning we must climb to its highest point," said the carpenter, "so for now we must rest." Many who were gathered near him said, "We cannot climb that mountain, for we shall have to leave behind the few possessions that we have. We have travelled many days to find this land of truth and peace, but we cannot leave behind all that we have brought with us."

The carpenter pondered upon the words they spoke and said that morning would bring to them the freshness of thought. The next day the carpenter led the pilgrims up upon the pathway that was at the side of the mountain.

As the day grew hot and long, so did many stop and say, "We come no further, for you are not the Holy One, we were mistaken." On the third day of his travel his feet were sore and weary was he to reach the land of his dream. Gathered only with him now were seven small children who had long ago, been orphaned and had no parents of their own. He looked at their tired little bodies and bid them to rest a while, for soon their journey would be over.

The evening grew dark and the night grew cold. Each child moved near him that they may keep warm. The carpenter pondered hard upon his dream and thoughts of confusion flowed within him. The next morning, upon sunrise, he awoke to see that in front of him was a valley of beauty that far surpassed his dreams. The children were not there and he began to worry at where they might be. He closed his eyes and asked that he might now be guided, for he had been fortold to come to the mountain he had climbed, but now he knew not what to do.

"My son," said a voice, "open your eyes and see." He looked way down into the valley of beauty and there was his little workshop and there were his seven children and his wife, who hurriedly was coming towards him. "How can this be?" said the carpenter.

"My son," said the voice, "you had a dream, your dream was a great journey. You set out upon your journey in life, bringing with you joy. You gave to each child in turn the truth of me. You set out one day from your home upon Earth to complete the vision that you had seen. You did so knowing you must go, leaving behind all that you loved upon Earth. When you set upon your last journey, it was to come home.

"You had seen the visions of my angels and knew that you must surpass the mountain of the Earth world to find me. When you sat upon the wayside, so did you leave behind your physical body. But, my son, you did not know that left upon the earth were your sons and daughter. They loved you and set out to find you. When they found your physical body, so did they grieve. But, my son, you know now the truth, that you

38

walked forwards towards the world of truth and peace, bringing your loved ones with you. Look again, my son."

This time the confusion within the carpenter's heart was great. And then he saw again his home and family. "You see," said the voice, "there is no end, the bond of love can never separate you from your loved ones. And as quick as the flickering of a flame, they shall be here also."

As the carpenter closed his eyes he fell into a deep sleep. When he awoke he walked back down the mountain and made his way home. When he arrived home there was no one there. Again he rose to confusion. "Please guide me," he called. "I know not what to do."

"My son," said the voice, "come back up the mountain." He climbed again to the top and this time all his family were there. "Oh, thank goodness," he said and embraced them all, "I thought I had lost you all."

A voice said to him, "My children of the Earth world, your life is only a dream, but when you pass from your physical bodies upon Earth, then do you come home. All that you were, upon all also do you bring. When you pass from your physical bodies you feel confusion because you do not understand that in my world you are born. You see now your loved ones.

"In your small moments of confusion were they too soon not with you?"

"There is no separation, only the flickering of a flame as you journey towards me. Joy upon Earth did you have, my son. Joy then upon death shall you receive, my son. For what you have sown so shall you reap. The passing from death to life takes many different roads. But you, my son, set out upon a journey to find me. You, my son, saw the visions of angels. You, my son, tried to help the many climb the mountain you climbed.

"You, my son, now understand truth."

THE FOUNTAINS OF WISDOM

Once, long ago, in the realms of eternity, lived a master who was the teacher of many things. In the realms of continued existence, there are many, many wonderful teachings for Mankind to find. There are, within the house of God, many rooms. When children of Earth have passed their teachings upon Earth, they take off their garments of Earth matter and knock upon the doors of their new teachings.

There was a child upon the Earth called Bella. She had lain many weeks sickly in her bed. Her mother and father loved her dearly and wished so much for the child to return to health. Bella, too, wished that she may be able to get up and play with the other children. But with the passing of time she accepted that for now she must rest and try and grow in strength. Bella spent many hours looking out of her small window near her bed.

She could just see the tops of the neighbouring houses and the hillside that led to a lake where many times her father and mother had taken her. Oh, how she had loved those days. She closed her eyes and wished so much that she was there. The thoughts of love flooded her mind, when very quietly she heard a voice, "Child," said the voice, "all things are possible if you try hard enough."

Bella opened her eyes and looked around the room, but could see no one. She closed her eyes again, thinking that perhaps she was dreaming, when again she heard a voice, "Child, all things are possible if you try." This time Bella kept her eyes closed and said, "Who are you?"

"I am the keeper of my father's children," the voice replied, "and work in His name that I may help those in need upon the Earth world. You may call me **Truth**," said the voice.

"Will you be my friend?" said Bella, "For so often I am lonely with the passing of time."

"Child," said the voice, "I have always been your friend, but never before have you been able to hear me. I speak to all children of the Earth, but only a few hear me."

"What do you do?" said Bella. "I answer the call within you in your times of need, that you may be led through the confusions of the Earth world."

"Can I see you?" said Bella. "You may, with the passing of time." Bella opened her eyes and no one was there. She closed her eyes and spoke, but no voice replied. Her mother came into the room and asked who she was talking to.

"I have a friend, Mother, but they do not live here, they live in God's house, the new place that we go to when we pass from Earth." Bella's mother was sorely puzzled that her child should speak of such things and worried that her health had grown worse.

"Please Bella, don't speak of such things, it is not healthy that you should think of death, nor that you should speak to people who are not here. Promise me that you will not do it again."

Bella tried to explain that all was well, but her mother would not listen. "All right mother, I won't talk to them again." With the passing of time Bella grew in strength and from her bed she walked now, downstairs, that she might be with her mother and father.

There were many toys and books for her to play with but within her she longed for the company of other children. During that day her mother had gone out to do some tasks and Bella sat in her chair thinking. As she closed her eyes, she heard a voice say, "Welcome my child, for now you grow in strength."

"Oh," said Bella, "you are my friend of Truth." "Yes," said the voice, "I have been near to you as always."

"My mother says it is wrong for me to speak to you, for my mind will not be healthy," said Bella.

"Child," said the voice, "I promise you the vistas of wisdom, far from whence I come, so shall you one day be."

"Well," said Bella, "we will meet in secret and you will teach me."

"Yes," said the voice, "I shall teach you who so want to know truth."

With the passing of time, Bella learnt many wonderful truths from her friend. And by now she called him "my Angel of Truth." Bella had learnt many of Earth's teachings and was now well in her health.

At the age of eighteen years, she set out upon the pathway of medicine, that she might be able to help many who were in need. With the passing of time she learnt many things until, at last, the skill of teaching was hers.

With the passing of years she had not listened to the voice of Truth, as time was so hard and much she had to do. It came now that she was to set out to a land where there were many sick who needed help.

She bid her family farewell and set off upon her great journey that lay across the sea. The journey was long and the seas were rough and great was Bella's fear. She felt so alone and wondered now if what she did was right, for she was destined to go amongst many sick people, in a land that she had only seen in a dream.

At last, the great voyage came to its end and Bella set off across the land to the many sick and needy. Upon her journey she had taken many oxen that were to carry her needs. There were, amongst the caravan of people, many servants who were of Greek origin. There were, amongst them, all many tanned people who were native to the country.

Amongst these people were many cultures and many superstitions. And to Bella they did not approve, for her skin was delicate and would seem to not be strong.

At night they all gathered together and held no regard for Bella. Soon the night grew dark and a great storm gathered around them. Many of the native people fell to the ground and were sorely afraid, for the spirit of the sky was angry.

Bella looked at the great skies rolling with the light of the storm and then pondered upon the many who were afraid. Just as she began to think on what she could do to help them, she heard a voice say, "Welcome, my child, you have called, that I may help."

"Oh," said Bella, rather startled that her thoughts were interrupted. "Child," said the voice, "I am the Angel of Truth, of whom you know. There are many here that need us this night."

Bella called to all the natives who were so afraid and said, "Come here my friends, sit by me, for I have no fear." The natives gathered near to where she was resting and looked at her with bewilderment, that her eyes were of no fear.

"Long ago," said Bella, "I was so afraid that I might die and leave my Earth life behind, but I had a friend who came to me and taught me much. The Angel of Truth gave to me a great wisdom and teaching, that I might grow in strength and fight my fears.

"As time passed, the duties of my Earth life did not permit me to see him quite so much. But now I have reached this time, in this land, much work must we do. If you all sit quietly I shall show you much that will still your minds and bring you truth."

The night grew darker and the storm grew in strength. Each man who gathered there drew close to Bella, for from around her glowed a strange light. Bella stood up, that she might be seen by all who were there.

"Now," said Bella, "you shall see." Bella closed her eyes and asked that the Angel of Truth may guide her as to what she must do.

Bella felt her eyes grow heavy and into a deep sleep she fell. The words from her mouth spoke.

"Oh children of the Earth world, fear not that I am here. To each of you is given an angel that in your times of need you may call." All the people gathered there watched as the light from Bella grew.

The storm of the night began to be cast away and all was still. Bella slowly came back from her sleep and all the native people had fallen into a peaceful sleep.

The next day they all set off upon the journey, but now the people who were so afraid seemed at peace and no longer did they leave Bella alone. Over the time of their journey, many times was Bella asked to tell to them stories, until at last they came to the end of their journey. Bella's days were spent tending the sick and lame and weary of that land, until Bella, at last, became very sick herself.

Now, many who had set out with Bella had stayed with her that they also may tend the sick, one of whom was full of love for Bella, with his dark eyes that glistened with joy at all Bella had taught him. His name was Ebra and his skin was dark. Ebra nursed and tended Bella day and night until her fever was over.

With the many passing years, Bella and Ebra became one, helping the sick and sharing the great teaching from the Angel of Truth, who many times came. It came to pass that in that time there was a great famine and rain was so sorely needed. Ebra grew sad from the sights that now befell his eyes that so many should be so hungry and lost.

He sat and thought about the years in which Bella had taught him about the Angel of Truth and now wondered at what he might do. Bella and Ebra had grown older in years and there was not much time left for them upon Earth.

44

As they sat together that night, many thoughts of love and truth did they exchange. Upon their awakening, much around them had changed. There were rivers and lush green banks with flowers that cascaded like waterfalls down upon the ground on which they sat. For a moment or two they looked at each other, bewildered at what they saw, until before them stood the Angel of Great Light. "Hello," said the angel. "Who are you?" said Bella and Ebra, "And where are we?"

"I promised you," said the angel, "that one day you should see me, for am I not the Angel of Truth? You set out, my children, upon a great journey, but now you have come home."

"Oh," said Bella, "but there is so much more for us to do and what of the great famine upon the Earth and all the people who need help. Surely there is more we should do?"

"My children," said the Angel of Truth, "each man is given what is for him to do, no more and no less. When your work is accomplished so do you return. But always there is another who is sent to continue their great journey and spread the help and love that is needed.

"For many Angels of Truth walk upon the Earth world, each doing what is for him to do. The day shall come that no more shall there be the sick, the lame, the weary and the sad. For each man shall know that, but in the flickering of a flame, he shall indeed walk in the Gardens of Peace.

"Until then, my children, many shall be born that shall speak with the tongues of angels. So peace be with you. Rest in the World of Truth. Until all Mankind shall one day wish to stay."

A FAR DISTANT LAND

There once was a child called Rebia who lived outside Syria, whose waters flowed towards the land of Egypt.

In Egypt there were many different people who had gathered from many of the surrounding countries. Amongst these people were many who had come from Syria. Now Rebia had many of her family who had long moved into the city of Judea, so long ago many of her family had gone to many different parts of the country.

There were many years that had passed and Rebia decided that she should go upon a journey from Judea, Syria into Egypt, that she may be able to find some of the family who had long ago been seen.

Her father and mother had passed from Earth life and Rebia now felt that the time had come in her life that she should try and find her brother, Joseph, whom she had not seen since she was a small child. He had set out many years ago to a far off distant land hoping to find the secret of life.

Rebia's mother and father had waited many years in hope that their son would return. Now the time had passed and Rebia felt she must try and find her brother. Off Rebia set, upon a mule that would help across the many valleys and mountains that her journey would take her upon. Rebia knew nothing of travel, but now, in her three score years of life, felt that she would be guided to the pathways that would lead her to her brother.

She set off just as the sun was rising and had felt that she should follow the rivers that flowed towards the east. Upon her journeying, the first day she felt sorely tired and wondered at how long she would have to travel in order that she might reach Egypt.

Upon her leaving Syria, it had meant she had to follow the river course; she indeed had to make a longer journey. But she felt so guided that she must do so. This meant that she firstly had to travel down country before she set up and across to Egypt. In a vision, Rebia had seen great pyramids and had heard her brother call many times.

Many years had passed but Rebia had held fast to her vision and had promised that one day she would do the bidding of her vision. Now the evening had grown dark and Rebia wondered at what part of the river she should cross when an old traveller appeared from across the water and called to her saying, "Cross my child, this is safe." Rebia gathered her mule and belongings together and crossed over the river towards the old traveller.

When she reached the other side quite safely, there appeared to be no traveller there. Rebia seemed puzzled and thought that perhaps the old traveller had gone on and was not journeying upon the same road as she. Many days passed and the river twisted and turned many pathways and Rebia grew tired of her journey. Upon the road she walked appeared many people, who were pilgrims on their way to the Holy Land, for in the city of Jerusalem they had heard of the coming of a great master.

Rebia listened with great interest that such a wonderful soul should be born. Now the city of David was many miles away and Rebia knew the days of travel must be long. Rebia loaded the mule and set off towards the temples of Egypt, looking now towards a large range of hills that she must cross. The night grew dark and Rebia became a little afraid as she climbed higher into the mountain range.

There came the time that the river made a division and Rebia wondered at what she should do. When she looked there was the old traveller. "Take the road to the east ,child," said the old traveller. "Oh thank you," said Rebia, but upon her glancing again at him he was not there. Rebia again seemed puzzled, but continued her journey along the river that flowed to the east.

When the break of daylight came, far off from the range of hills, she could see the rivers of Jordia that flowed down in the Nile that would lead her now into Egypt. When she reached the river Jordan there were many who passed her who had heard of the birth of a great Messiah, so they too were going to the city of David, for Jerusalem showed to them a great star.

Rebia bid them farewell and continued onwards towards the River Nile until at last came the vista of pyramids. Upon her reaching Egypt, she searched for her brother, Joseph, but nowhere could he be found. She consulted many wise men who were brethren to the temple of Ala and asked that they may guide her. "Go back," they said, "and search for your brother in Judea."

Rebia could not face the thought of that journey alone and asked that she may be given a band that she may join, but none were travelling to Judea. The time came that she set out back along the journey that she had taken. Rebia grew older in time and weary but as she neared the end of her journey there appeared the old traveller. "Weary not my child," said he, "for soon you shall find your brother Joseph."

That night Rebia rested and joined a band of pilgrims who were journeying to the Holy Land. They spoke of a great Messiah who had been sent to the city of David. Rebia decided that she should join this band of pilgrims and set off that day to see the Holy Land. Upon their arrival it had taken them much time and Rebia no longer felt she should find her brother, Joseph. They had heard that the Messiah was in the city of Jerusalem and that he was now two years of age.

They came upon the house of the Messiah and knocked upon the door. As the door opened then did Rebia see her brother, Joseph. Oh, the great reunion. Rebia could not understand, for she had come to see the Messiah and there was her brother. Now, standing in the shadows of the doorway was the old traveller, who called to her saying, "You set out upon a journey to find your brother. You were led across the rivers, the mountains and into many lands.

"When you were so weary, yet again you had to journey back, each time you were led, that you may see the strength needed was faith. Within the cities you have walked, you have gained knowledge and wisdom. Now you walk a road that has led you to the Messiah. Your brother is the son of God, you are the son of God. Each man is the son of God. To you this day is given a truth, that you may lead the pilgrims of the Earth world to find their brothers, that they too will see. The Great Messiah comes many times. To you, who travel the Earth with faith in your searching, shall be given the door that you may find the truth.

AWAKEN THY SOUL

Long ago, in the World of Great Light, lived many wise souls. They had lingered within the vineyards of truth for many eons, of time in order that their **light** may indeed become so bright. A few had ventured many times towards the Earth world in order that they may guide the souls of physical matter onto a pathway that would lead them to the world that one day they should all come.

It came to pass that many of the great souls of light looked upon the dense darkness that surrounded planet Earth and wondered at what they might do to help lift the great coat of ignorance away from the Earth children. There was a great meeting called and great counselling took place. There were many masters from many levels that lay within our Father God's vineyards.

The counselling began, the brothers of truth spoke to the masters of wisdom and great was their compassion for planet Earth. That day a great allegiance was made between many of the spheres that lay within the world of **Eternal Light**.

There was formed, from that day, a pledge that a certain number of the great souls of light may join together, completing a circle of great light and as joined together they would become one.

The great brothers of light were to become The White Brotherhood. The light from them was to be given to the children of the Earth world in order that through that great light would pour through truth and teachings. The order of the truth was that each child met on Earth would be able, by their light, to gather great strength in their teachings towards the Earth world. With this great strength given, then would the darkness of the Earth world become lifted away.

50

It was a difficult task that The White Brotherhood set out upon, for they had to become indeed joined that they may penetrate the veils of the Earth world's vibration.

As the aeons of time passed, so this great allegiance went forward, each brother betrothing his light to the other in order that the work may succeed. The Lodge of Great Light became sought after in the Realms of Great Light and so many more joined forces in helping The Brotherhood of Mankind.

After many, many Earth years had passed, so did the children of the Earth world begin to see the light that was being transmitted towards the veil of darkness that surrounded that the Earth. Gradually the great battle of light and darkness was fought.

There were many children upon the Earth who saw the light of truth and so were then many great teachings given. As the time passed, so did the Great White Brotherhood accomplish much in the name of Fatherhood of Mankind. The teachings of Spirit availed a great truth. And many within The Lodge became teachers to the children of the Earth world. And so did the veil of light interpenetrate the souls of the Earth world, who were awakened.

In the passing of time The Brotherhood of Light was able to give safe passage to the many who needed help upon the Earth world. The Lodge grew in strength and great walls of knowledge and wisdom were opened wide for the children of the Earth world to receive teachings. It came to pass that within the spheres their work grew and the Circle of Brotherhood joined together with yet another and another, until their light and teachings gathered more and more strength.

Their mission was now vast and as their strength grew so did the light upon the Earth world grow. The filtering of their knowledge was now given by their nearness and by the Earth's willingness to learn. The masters of wisdom took aside many upon the Earth and taught them great truth.

Each child upon the Earth, pledged an allegiance with the Fatherhood of Mankind and set out upon a journey on planet Earth and spread the great light of truth within the Earth world herself. Now, within the passing of time, many have now joined the Great White Brotherhood and so shall it be that, from strength to strength, the great void of darkness shall be fought and conquered.

Each child who walks within the teachings of truth shall throw their soul open and say, "I enter, brothers, out of love. I betroth my soul to the wisdom of truth. In order that I may become one with our father, our mother, our brothers and our sisters of love. Give unto me now **light**, that I too may lift The Sword of Truth and smite the battles of Ignorance, in order that thy Great Lodge may be built upon the Earth."

Child, may God bless thee, keep thee and sustain thee, as thee wield the sword of light.

THE POOLS OF CLEANSING

Long ago, in the city of Rome, there was an emperor called Nichodemus.

He was a mighty and powerful man, who ruled his kingdom in order to acquire wealth. Within him lay no peace, for he gave no peace; to all he met he made his commands for the day, working such servant to his utmost. There were many cruel sports that gave him great pleasure through the day.

It came to pass in the city of Rome that there was to be a great feasting; many people gathered in order that they may join the great festivities of the day. As the evening drew nigh, great sights were to be seen and many gathered within the city square.

It came to pass that a stranger drew near unto the city. He had come from the land of Israel and was travelling to spread the words of truth, preparing the way for the coming of the great Messiah. With his garments clad around him and his tired feet, he showed great signs of his wearying journey. He sat beside the water well in the centre of the square.

He bent forward in order to cup a drink from the well, as much was his thirst. From behind him sprang two Roman soldiers, who seized him by his robe and took him to a small crowd who had been gathered together. All the people were then lead into the Roman arena, for great was their need for sport.

"Why are we here?" asked the traveller. One young girl replied, "Because we wear the sign of the great master Jesus and Christians are much hated here."

"But," said the traveller, "many prophets have come upon our lands and great shall be the coming of many more. The Master Jesus walks the Earth within the Holy Lands. We come only to prepare his way with love."

The young girl threw herself within the arms of the traveller and said, "We know of these things, but within my heart now I am afraid." The traveller took her to his arms and said, "Be strong of faith my child and your armour shall surely save you; none can penetrate its radiance."

That night great battles were fought and many Christians died. The traveller sat with the young girl awaiting their time of torture, but morning broke and showed that many who had been *amused* with the games had fallen asleep. The old traveller then quietly walked with the young girl across the arena.

Oh, so sad were the sights of the innocent people who lay within its walls.

The traveller walked onwards, leading the young girl with him. The guards were long asleep with their great pleasures. Out through the city they went, until at last they were safe within the hills.

The young girl was crying and much sadness filled the traveller's heart. They stopped beside the edge of a small stream in order that they may drink.

"Come now," said the traveller, "drink and bathe within this water." They bent forward in order that they may freshen themselves, then they noticed the figure of a man reflected in the water. They turned around, wondering if it was the Roman soldiers.

"Be at peace," said the man. The traveller and the young girl then fell into a deep sleep.

Into the pool they went, the colour of great beauty cascading upon them. They swam through the water out onto a vast land of 'light'. There were many people there in the glistening robes of colours.

"Welcome children," said a soul of great light. "You come this day that we may refresh thy soul, for your garments of light have been sorely tried."

Off in the distance there were many souls, all being bathed in the pools of cleansing. The traveller asked who they were and the soul of great light replied, "Did you not see them, my son, lying within the hatred of the Roman arena?"

"Yes," said the traveller, "and much sadness did we feel." The soul of great light said, "My children of the Earth world, you who walk in the name of God. You who are persecuted for your thoughts of love and truth, see that thy armour of love can never be destroyed. See that if thy life physically ends, that none can sever that love. For you are the immortal sons of God. Upon thy passing all suffering shall be washed away, all wounds shall be repaired, for your Father refreshens **all** that the trials of the Earth give unto thee.

"This day, my children, you too have been cleansed and replenished in order that you may travel the Earth world, preparing the way for the coming of truth."

The traveller awoke and the young girl was smiling. "How beautiful was my dream," she said. But the stranger who stood by the pool said, "Child, it was no dream. For surely you must know that goodness and mercy shall follow thee all the days of thy life. The gift of love is great, thy armour of **faith** can never be destroyed, for all the Pools of Cleansing shall replenish thee.

"Upon thy road in life and upon thy birth into the Realms of Eternal Life, the hand of Mankind may wound thee, the hatred of Mankind may smart thee, but the Hand of Our Father shall save thee.

"Go forward this day with thy Armour of Faith."

REBECCA'S LOVE

Once, long ago, in the city of Jerusalem, lived a family of Greek Jews. Although they were of Greek origin it was their forefathers who had travelled to this land where they now lived.

Rebecca was the youngest child of three; she had one sister, Orenia and a brother, Orthous. Her sister, Orenia, had married and had fine children of her own and her brother, Orthous, had long ago set out to find his way in life, tilling the land and helping wherever he could find work.

Rebecca's mother was sorely lame and could do little to help within the house, so often, as a small child, Rebecca did the daily chores, which then enabled her father to go out upon his search for work. The days within Rebecca's life were days of great poverty for many. The serfs of the Earth world were expected to glean for their food or to beg within the market square.

It came to the time that Rebecca must bring into the house food, in order that they may survive, for her mother now was much lamer and sick in health and her father's age was well upon him. Rebecca set out that morning to glean within the fields of harvest. She held around herself a garment in order that each grain may be placed safely within.

The day was long and hot and her back became weary from its bending. Amongst the many who had joined her she noticed a young boy, who also had wearied of his work. They decided to rest a while beneath the shade of a large Judas tree. During their time of conversation Rebecca had made a dear friend called Esram.

Esram was a fine looking young man and Rebecca held his love within her heart with great joy. She walked towards her home in order that the food for the day may be shared. But on her way she saw a stranger laying by the wayside, great were his wounds. She stopped and placed her gleaning down upon the ground and tended to the wounds; she ran off in order to collect some water to moisten the sick man's lips.

Upon her return, the poor soul had died. Rebecca sat beside him and great were her tears, for it saddened her that no one should care upon his passing. Rebecca then noticed that her garment was gone and food should not be able to be taken home. She gently laid a small cover of flowers over the old man and said a small prayer that he should find his way home to the land of God.

When Rebecca arrived home her father and mother were awaiting their vitals for the day. Rebecca was sorry that there was no food and sad within her heart to see the hunger within her parent's eyes. After the evening had passed so then did the stars of the night shine, so Rebecca collected her garments and went out into the night to glean from the field of that day.

Upon her arrival she saw her young friend Esram and asked what he was doing. Esram explained he had no home, that he took shelter wherever he could and that Mother Earth always looked after him. Rebecca told Esram of her day and how she had been sad that a person should die and yet not be missed upon the Earth.

Esram told her that she was not to be sad, because the land of God was far more beautiful than the Earth. As the days and months passed, Esram and Rebecca's love grew. They worked hard together in order that they may eat. It came to pass that Rebecca's mother and father passed into the world of Holy Spirit. Rebecca was sad for her love for them was great, but Esram had so often spoken of the beautiful world of God that she knew their passing would bring them great joy.

Over the years that followed, Rebecca and Esram lived as man and wife. Hard were their days to survive but great was the love that lay between them. It came to the day that Esram had grown old and it was nearing the time for him to go into the world of Spirit. Rebecca sat beside Esram's bed and great sorrow befell her Earth heart.

"Oh my Father God, teach me to know thee, teach me that I may know the plane of your ways." Rebecca bent her head as her beloved Esram passed into his awaiting life. So great were the tears of Rebecca as she held onto the memories of her beloved.

The days and weeks that followed were of great confusion and anger, for now within her heart was only a desolate loneliness. Rebecca had become ill and lay within her bed.

She closed her eyes and asked that she too may die, that she may go to the World of God. But unto Rebecca appeared a vision. "My child," said the voice, "do not throw away thy life, do not try and leave thy physical body before thy time is given. For you upon the Earth do many things for me. You live that I may be seen in all you do. You live that I may talk with thee, in order that my breath may breathe the truth of love.

"Lift up thy weary body, let your soul so shine that I may be seen again. The gift of love is for you to share, I take not that love away, but I give to thee much love that you may share it with many. Do all with this thought, honour thy mother, thy father, thy sister and thy brother, for when you come home great treasures shall you find within my house.

"For love does not die, but it grows from your physical birth to your physical death. The soul of you is fed until it becomes the great light that shall shine within my house of love forever. Upon thy passing great beauties of truth shall you see. Your beloveds are forever awaiting the great reversion."

58

THE GARDEN OF TRUTH
(Written for The Dark Night of Thy Soul)

There once was a little girl who found a beautiful garden full of lovely flowers. Such beauty filled this little garden that she wished with all her heart it was hers. Upon her enquiries, she found that the gardener who tended to its beauties was indeed a very kindly person and their knowledge of the beauty within the garden was great.

During the sunny days the little girl frequently visited the beautiful garden and asked the gardener who tended it, if it may be hers. The gardener replied, "All that is within her my little child is for you to tend as you may." So the little girl gladly took the gift of the beautiful garden.

But the seasons changed and no longer did she visit the garden, for with the passing of time she began to grow and there were the gardens of life to tend to. Within her youth the young girl grew and much knowledge did she gain within her life and often the memories of her beautiful garden drove her onwards to fight many of the turmoils that fell upon her.

Then fell upon the youth of this child a great illness; she fell upon a sleep state and could not awaken from the dream of life. She purged within her mind for it to stop, she ran from the thoughts of herself for fear that they may consume her. The confusions of her life threw her as though tossed upon a stormy sea. Then came a small voice within her confusion that bade her to go into the beautiful garden. The young girl had become afraid of her very knowing; no longer was she even sure of the truth within her thoughts.

She awoke one morning and the turbulent sea had ceased and she felt a small calmness within her. And again the voice bade her to go to the garden of beauty. With her tormented confusion, she walked as if upon paper towards the garden she had known.

And there before her stood the truth. Oh the sadness within her heart was great, for there were the beautiful flowers, choking with the weeds of ignorance. There were the fences to this beautiful garden blown to the winds of mortal wounds. And there was the gate to this garden blowing backwards and forwards as a season of time that had long been forgotten.

She stood there naked to the truth, to the truth that she had been given a gift, that she would tend daily to its needs. She fell upon her knees and was naked to the truth of herself. So long had she held onto the thoughts of doubt, anguish and fear that she had buried the gift of love.

She cried out to be forgiven and great truth did she see. Within the cries of her truth then did the gardener appear. "Oh child, you have returned after your seasons of growing. Do not be sad, for if you had not been lost how could you have returned? For if you are given a gift too easily, you see how it may be forgotten. Too easily you see that it may become saturated with the thoughts of time. So, my child, I will help you build this garden and we will tend it together; each day we will meet until the fence is mended that it will weather any storm. Each weed will be cast away that the flowers may breathe and spread their great array. And the soil, my child, we will turn until it shall glimmer through all seasons. And the gate shall be fastened that no man may pull from the garden the beauty that we make. Each time a small repair is needed so shall we do it together and child, when the flowers are brimming over so shall we pick them and share the beauty of our garden.

"May God go with you."

A NOTE FROM THE AUTHOR

It is plain to see, as the time has passed, the many different aspects of our spiritual unfolding.

There are many avenues that you may enter, where you shall be called upon, to wave the gift of knowledge wisely.

Your armour of light shall be lifted into the heights of immortality and so shall your mortal mind throw thy soul into the pits of confusion.

The day of 'The Dark Night of Thy Soul' shall indeed make you climb the mountains of truth in order that you may become a soldier of light, no more to allow thy mortal mind to throw you upon the mortal mind of self.

When you return from the valleys of confusion, then do you become one with thy soul. For thy shield of light may be used in the name of truth, thy sword may wield against the darkness of self and thy crown may shine with wisdom in order that thy truth may walk with The light of God.

Annabelle Lee-Botting

NEW TEACHINGS FROM CHEAM

THE GIFT OF PEACE

"Be at peace, oh child," cried a still small voice from within, "for great has your battle been and great victory is now. You wandered off into a far distant land and found sorrow and anguish within your heart; the darkness within your mind threw you into the pits of confusion upon the plains of thy physical mind. But now, my daughter of light, sit upon the throne of spiritual comfort and I shall teach thee."

Long ago, at the beginning of time, there were many days of darkness within the mind of Man. Then Mankind began to strive for truth and so to the Earth world came great light that he may be shown a way, the way back from whence he came. There were many who came in many disguises, each giving the gifts that were for him to give.

The gifts are given in many ways - in the toiling upon the land, in the creative mind, in the service to your fellow man. All these gifts are but the cup of sharing.

Now, many great seers have come to the Earth world through the time of man, some to serve in the synagogues, many who were called saints after their departure from physical matter. But the most important thing for each to know is that you but serve the purpose for you to fulfil.

Dear children, when you come to the Earth world as young, then you are given only that that you may do. But as you grow in strength, knowledge and knowing, then do you turn toward the road of higher attainment. In your responsibilities then does your temple become purified and filled with the wine of truth. There in your temple of truth lie many riches that are for you to know and to give.

So you walk within the rhythm of life, serving, giving and doing all that you do upon your pathway of progression.

This is a hard time, for you are now grown and the responsibility becomes then yours. For knowledge and truth has to be held with great love.

The temple is sacred ground and must be cleansed with **Peace**. When in the valleys of peace, then you must walk out amidst the storms of life, knowing as the winds of life toss many this way and that way that your temple of truth and wisdom shall be greatly used. So, as the keeper of the gate, you walk forward, holding the key with love.

The responsibility is truth unto your ownself and truth outflowing to all you meet. Peace must prevail you, even though you may be cast upon the storms of Earth and faith shall cast away the anguish that many would pull your temple down with.

Now, look my beloveds, the key to all is Peace. For peace within brings peace without. Love within shall feel no pain. Faith shall smite the mind of self and great shall be thy Temple of Truth. Great shall be thy service to thy fellow man.

The responsibility grows as the temple is purified, cleansed and renewed, that the wine that flows from thy Father may flow through thee to thy fellow man.

THY COAT OF TRUTH

When the voice of God is heard within the heart of man, then does he search for a great truth.

The coat of his mortal mind is thrown away as the coat of ignorance is revealed.

Many times he will search within his heart, saying, "Please show me which way I must go." Always he is guided, although he may feel he walks alone and becomes afraid of the path he walks.

But my beloveds of the Earth world, thy armour of light shall lead you forward; let thy mortal doubt be cast away into the wilderness. Pick up thy shield that is truth. Hold firm thy sword of faith.

The light of thy Father shall feed to thee the bread of life, the wine of love until you shall become as the lambs of the world that shall lead in simplicity the great love that you have found.

That many shall graze upon the rich pastures. And many shall receive the blessings of light.

THE FOUNTAINS OF TRUTH

"Blessed are the pure in heart for they shall inherit the Kingdom of Heaven," said the wise man who came to Earth. He taught all to look within the doors of love to find the kingdom that all Mankind seeks to find. They look for the truth in all material life and seek to see the solidarity of where it may be.

They say if only we could have proof then no more would they wonder about the many teachings that the wise men bring. But dear children of the Earth world, the Master Jesus taught all to enter within to find the truth of God. For our Father God sees all. There is not one thing that is not known, not one soul is not seen. For the One Who Loves All, then is All.

When the many seers and saints cometh unto the Earth world, they do these things because they see the Kingdom of Heaven within their daily lives. They do not take upon themselves coats of greed. They do not take upon themselves goals of fame. But they take upon themselves great truth, in order that they may walk into the gardens of truth.

In their seeking, many times their truths are tested, in order that they may grow in light. Within the mind of Mankind is the mortal eye of his soul. He will have to walk forward serving his physical life, in order that he may grow, to enter the sanctuary of truth. The fountains of wisdom will feed to him much.

And many times the fountains of truth shall bring to him a time of change. For many times he will feel the roads of his physical growth and he will fall upon his knees and say, "Oh Father guide me, Father help me." And often times he will feel his Father does not hear him. But I say unto you that all is known, all is answered. But the time of growing must be in order that the temple of light may grow.

Many times the wayfarers of the Earth world sit and rest a while before they journey any further. And in their resting they grow and in the travelling they indeed see the life of the Earth.

When the Master Jesus came to the Earth world, he came knowing there would be times that he would grow. Times that he may rest. Times that his physical self would be sorely tested.

But when he surmounted the Mount of Olives, he did so knowing the Kingdom of Heaven would lead all Mankind home.

Upon the passing of time many have come to the Earth world to teach. Many have come to serve, many have come to love and give a service unto their fellow man. But to all who walk the pathway towards the Fountains of Truth, I say unto you: Your tomorrows will be victorious unto your Father God.

If you render a service of love then all else shall be added unto you and the Kingdom of Heaven shall shine like a star within the Earth world.

A POEM FROM ANNABELLE

The subdued thoughts of mind, bring past pain forgot and gone.
I long only now for now, as life and love entwine.
The yesterdays of tormented dreams are softly put away.
My thoughts of dreams untold, will reveal themselves, one day.
The mind of stress and thoughts of pain, hid 'away my light'.
I awoke it seems, from all those dreams.
And stood and looked and saw, a warrior, I now must be, and slay
those thoughts, and say 'no more'.
All is conquered here I stand, my 'light still dimly lit'.
But now I say to dreams of mind, now stand with me, and 'sit'.
Because our dreams of life as real, can no longer be.
For you my mind, must stand a while, whilst my 'light' see 'Victory'.
When this is done, the way is clear, and glorious shall it be.
For fear and doubt we have cast out, and you and I shall see.
The light within shall feed you peace, and confidence shall reign.
And what was once a painful thing, shall all the 'light proclaim'.
No more to cry unfair within, you will feel no pain.
So walk with me dear mind of mine, and see how far we go.
And then I look and you will see, we have slain all 'ego'.
Man will think how fine we are, how well we are in control.
And they will never know the road we walked, towards the final goal.
For victory is ours indeed, but, 'Oh, the death of mind'.
To slay the very thought of fear, that 'almost made us blind'.
But light within, is now a 'Flame', that is well hid from Man,
but God stood 'As Our Friend', as we worked through 'His Plan'.